UBUNTU AND THE WORD

UBUNTU AND THE WORD

REV. COREY BROWN

WRITEONTIME

CONTENTS

Acknowledgments

ACKNOWLEDGMENTS

I dedicate this book to the Afrodiaspora, to all the marginalized and oppressed who wonder if there is more to understanding their faith. If you are a believer, this book is for you. Whether you are a believer, questioning your beliefs, have left the faith, practice another faith, or identify as an atheist—this book is for you. Yes, this book is based on Christian scripture. Still, I submit that the African Diaspora must be allowed, enabled, and empowered to see itself within the Sacred. We must see ourselves not only as part of the Imago Dei but as the Imago Dei itself.

I dedicate this book to my seminary professors and fellow seminarians at McAfee School of Theology, who opened my eyes to a new world that already existed but was new nonetheless. In this new world, I went from knowing a lot about a petty, trifling god to knowing so little about an awe-inspiring God. I allowed myself to let go of what I thought I knew without question and embrace the unknown, the *mysterium tremendum* and the *mysterium fascinosum* that are the Creator.

I dedicate this book to my Afrodiasporan pastor and preacher colleagues. Although the last several years since the election of the forty-fifth President of the United States have been more challenging than we expected, you persevere. You must stand before the people and preach Sunday after Sunday through times of social and racial injustice, political unrest and upheaval, police violence against Black bodies, a global pandemic, and, worse yet, the era of white mainstream Eurocentric evangelicalism. Yes, it feels like we are on the Temptations' Ball of

Confusion hurtling toward the sun rather than on the Earth revolving around it. You have understood that it is not about compromising your beliefs but always seeing if they align with Jesus' teachings of love found throughout the Gospel. The late Bishop Carlton Pearson showed us that love is essential to our faith, even at the expense of rejection and expulsion.

I dedicate this book to my parents, siblings, and children. As I write, you have been my muse, hoping to convey to you and the world that there is a better way to approach our faith, especially our scripture. I want you to understand and be okay with the notion that all there is to know about God and our relationship with God is not contained in a book, even if it is designated as "Holy." I want you all to know that I love you and only want what is best for you as you move through this "thing called life."[1]

Finally, I dedicate this book to Cheryl, my wife, who always encourages me to follow the voice of God and to walk in my calling, even if she could not see the vision God gave me. I will be honest: the vision was not always clear to me, but I knew God was telling me to move, much like the story of Abraham leaving his homeland with nothing but his family and all they could carry with no set destination. Cheryl, you have been my partner in ministry and one of my biggest cheerleaders. I thank you, and I love you, Gorgeous.

[1] *Prince and the Revolution – Let's Go Crazy*, accessed November 29, 2023, https://genius.com/Prince-and-the-revolution-lets-go-crazy-lyrics.

CHAPTER ONE

Introduction

***

"Just as the Christian religious practices and biblical scripture are not the entirety of the faith, the Afrodiasporan Corporeal and Spiritual Beginnings should not be restricted to the era of the European Trans-Atlantic Slave trade."
-Rev. Corey L. Brown, MDiv

***

Greetings and Grand Risings to you, my fellow Afrodiasporic friends and family. I am Rev. Corey L. Brown, MDiv (https://www.writeon-time.llc), also known as "The Woke Heretic." As a heretic, I believe my task or charge is to continuously challenge all notions that I or anyone else knows everything there is to know about Christianity, including its sacred scripture, the Bible. When we read sacred scriptures, we should do so with a critical side-eye because we must question why we think scripture says what it says. It is not just about being able to remember and recite scripture ad nauseam. Scripture was not created ex nihilo. Scripture, be it the Buddhist Tripitaka, the Hindu Upanishads, the Muslim Qur'an, the Jewish Torah, or the Christian Bible, each has its own origin story.

I also adopted the term *woke* because I believe being *woke* means you are in a constant state of skepticism, like that of Jesus' disciple,

Thomas, who earned the moniker of "Doubting Thomas." A better name for him might be "Woke Thomas." He was the brave one seeking proof rather than unquestioningly believing what people told him. As the saying goes, "Believe half of what you see, none of what you hear." Thomas embodied this principle. Sometimes, our eyes can fool us, so we must look beyond what we see and question why we see what we see.

I am an Afrodiasporic Spiritual Engineer and a proud member of the African Diaspora or the Afrodiaspora collective. Throughout this book, I use the terms "African Diaspora" and "Afrodiaspora" interchangeably, as I believe these terms are much more inclusive and representative of the beautiful tapestry of Black peoples in the Western Hemisphere. The term "African American" carries the connotation of being limited to the people who are descendants of enslaved Africans in the United States.

UBUNTU

Before delving into topics such as theologies and hermeneutics, exploring the term UBUNTU and its significance to the Afrodiaspora is essential. UBUNTU, a term with African origins, can be traced back to the beginning—the Creation story. When *YHWH* was creating the first human, *YHWH* deemed it unfit for the first human to be alone. Even before the creation of the second human, *YHWH* highlighted the concept of UBUNTU. UBUNTU is a communal term. The blessing bestowed upon the first humans to be fruitful and multiply exemplified UBUNTU (Genesis 1). Similarly, when *YHWH* blessed Abram and Sarai and told them they would birth nations and their children would be as numerous as the stars in the sky, this was UBUNTU (Genesis 15,17). The promise to Abraham and Hagar that Ishmael would be fruitful and exceedingly numerous also embodied UBUNTU (Genesis 17).

The origin of the word and concept of UBUNTU is attributed to the Bantu people and their phrase, *"umuntu ngumuntu ngabantu,"* which in Zulu means "a person is a person through other people."[1]

For me, this truly captures the essence of what it means to be a part of the beautiful tapestry we call humanity. There is an interdependency, a mutuality that is unavoidable for humans and the rest of Creation. We must understand that things that impact us impact the rest of Creation, and vice versa. One-third of our food crops require cross-pollination, indicating that bees are a critical part of the world's ecosystem. This means that factors affecting the bee population will influence the ability of the human population to feed itself.[2] Embedded within the phrase is the Bantu metaphysical concept of personhood in life and the afterlife.

The modern-day understanding of UBUNTU is credited to the South African concept of "I am because you are" and "You are because we are." All thanks go to Bishop Desmond Tutu for popularizing UBUNTU as a global term. UBUNTU is different from theology because it is more of an African humanist philosophical term.

UBUNTU is a term for the community, embodying a reciprocal relationship between us: "I am because you are" and "You am because I am." It also includes the concepts "I am because we are" and "We are because I am." This forms the inseparable, inescapable premise of community. I would also submit that UBUNTU was established at the beginning of humanity. The Creator created a mate for the first human because He felt that man should not have to live in solitude. This implies that we do not exist solely for ourselves; our being depends upon the being of others, and vice versa. Bishop Desmond Tutu frequently used the South African term to describe a means to an end. UBUNTU is the means to the end—the Beloved Community. UBUNTU is also about fulfilling the Second Greatest Commandment: loving your neighbor as you love yourself.

I opened this chapter with a quote that explains that the spiritual or even Christian beginnings of the African people did not start with the first encounters with the European enslavers/colonizers. One of the goals of this book is to reclaim something bestowed upon us through what Frank Thomas sees as the combination of the "theological and the rhetorical."[3] Although his frame of reference is Afrodiasporan preaching, I will look at this union through the lens of "the readers, the hearers, and the doers of God's Holy Word." In the first chapter of the book of James, we are told not just to be hearers of the word but also doers. I want to add that we should embody the Word through our being, through UBUNTU. Our faith journeys are not just about doing but about being, about being fully who God created us to be.

Our ancestors worshipped the Creator of the heavens and the earth centuries before people of European descent set foot on African soil, as evidenced by the story of Moses' marriage to an Ethiopian woman and Philip's encounter with the Ethiopian Eunuch. In this case, Ethiopia was not necessarily limited to the present-day borders of the country of Ethiopia. Still, it did mean there were ties with the continent of Africa, with the Blackness that is Africa.

As a pastor/minister, the most crucial part of one's calling is caring and feeding of the souls of the individuals under one's care. I like the analogy of flight attendants giving the passenger count to the pilot before takeoff. The flight attendant tells the pilot how many "souls" are embarked for the flight, not how many "people." When entrusted with the responsibility of someone's soul, one should take what they are doing a little more seriously. I also adopted the engineer role as a nod to my science background. An engineer designs, builds, and maintains something. Through intelligent design, a spiritual engineer connects with the Creator and Creation, builds or crafts a message for the people under their charge, and works towards maintaining the communal vision for the people.

We spend an excessive amount of time in the realm of religiosity. This book's goal is to create a balance between religiosity and spirituality. Religiosity revolves around the customs, traditions, doctrine, and dogma of our religious institutions, encompassing all tangible components of our beliefs. On the other hand, spirituality delves into the transcendent, focusing on something greater than oneself with an intellectual component. Deep within, *YHWH* has implanted an innate curiosity within us, a perpetual desire that there must be more, that there has to be more. We should strive to be in a constant state of discovery, constantly evolving our beliefs. Even the first human beings believed there was more. This is what drove them to eat the forbidden fruit: curiosity. "There has to be more."

The Bible is unquestionably one of the most excellent books ever written. However, I also contend that the Bible is one of the most misunderstood and misinterpreted books ever written. My faith is founded on my belief that scripture is divinely inspired. Many people have different ideas about what divinely inspired means. For a point of reference, divinely inspired does not mean that God dictated the Bible to its authors or handed the book down to individuals. I understand divine inspiration to be that the authors were filled with the Spirit while chronicling the story of a particular group of people in a particular part of the world at particular periods of time. This is called context, and context is essential. My faith is also grounded in many other things not found within the binding of the canon of scripture we call the Bible. I love the Christian faith and its church, but I am much more a lover of humanity, Creation, and the Creator.

I am not writing this book to suggest that the Bible and its teachings should be discarded but rather to help us develop a healthier, more holistic relationship with scripture. The purpose of this book is to serve as a bridge between everyday religious discourse and religious academia. *UBUNTU and the Word* will provide enough substance to help build a solid biblical foundation for the average layperson while helping the religious academic understand the layperson's approach to reading and studying the Bible. The layperson will learn or better understand how to exegete a scriptural text properly. Simultaneously, the academic will learn or better understand the layperson's religious praxis as it relates to the Bible. The layperson will gain a better understanding of the origins of the canon of scripture we call the Bible, while the academic professional will gain insights into the societal challenges of scripture reading for the untrained and possibly acquire better skills in interacting with the general populace, especially the Afrodiaspora.

Why do I specifically mention *Western Christians*? This is because even though the United States' founders fought for independence, it is apparent that the country still clings to all things European, specifically those associated with whiteness. If you pay attention to commercials or the replies from our smart devices, you'll notice that the voices often have British accents. There is even a fascination with the lives of British Royalty. Christianity in the Western world is heavily steeped in Eurocentrism. Those pursuing postgraduate degrees in the Christian religion must read German and/or French, in addition to the biblical languages, to understand and study the commentaries and teachings of European biblical scholars and theologians. Even the founder of Protestantism, Martin Luther, was German. In predominantly white seminaries, your education would not be complete without studying white male European theologians like Karl Barth, Dietrich Bonhoeffer, Paul Tillich, Karl Rahner, Jürgen Moltman, H. Richard Niebuhr, or Reinhold Niebuhr.[4] White male European theologians seemingly constitute the primary source of Christian theology. While many Western Christians may not be European, our understanding of the Bible is rooted in a Western Eurocentric postmodern viewpoint.

There is little mention of Latinx, Feminist, Womanist, African, or African American theologians or scholars, which may cast these specific theologians as illegitimate simply because they do not conform to the white male Eurocentric mold. Notably, Black scholars and theologians like James Deotis Roberts, James Cone, Katie Geneva Cannon, Cain Hope Felder, Mitzi Smith, Ralph Basui Watkins, Wil Gafney, Esau McCauley, Chanequa Walker Barnes, Angela Parker, Pamela Lightsey, Kelly Brown Douglas, and Lisa Fields play significant roles within Black theological spaces.

The Bible, as commonly understood in the United States, is often approached through the lens of what Toni Morrison calls the "White Gaze." This perspective, one of the many lenses through which we interpret the world, has deeply conditioned even members of the African Diaspora to view all things through the paradigm of the White Gaze.[5] Linda James Myers, Ph.D., writes that there is a reluctance, even resistance, within Western societies to appreciate or acknowledge African or Afrodiasporan worldviews. Recognizing that we never read the Bible in a vacuum is crucial. At this time, the world is grappling with successive global crises exacerbated by the COVID pandemic. We find ourselves amid environmental, sociological, ecological, political-economic, and moral upheavals.[6] This poses a significant challenge, as it compels individuals like me, a middle-aged Black man in a post-Christendom, post-truth United States, to read a scripture written in one context through the lens of another, one that lies outside the context of my social location.

The name *Jesus* is a German transliteration of the Hebrew name *Yeshua*. Similarly, the name *Yahweh* is a German transliteration of *YHWH*, originally intended to be the unpronounceable name of the Creator. Many Bible commentaries we use are heavily rooted in Eurocentrism. So, how do we address this? When we encounter challenges in our lives, it often helps us to step away from the problem and try to shift our perspective. Notably, the Christian faith is not named for Yeshua, his God-given name; it is named for his title, "the Christ." *YHWH* had nothing to do with the name "*Christ*." *Christ* was not even His last name but a title for the role he fulfilled. This means that if the name of our religion is not derived from its namesake, we may need to reconsider how we approach the religion, its practices, and especially its scriptures.

Christ is derived from the Greek word "*christos*" and the Hebrew word "*meshiah*," both meaning "Anointed One." In light of this, Christianity is a religious tradition that should be based on following the works and the teachings of the Anointed One, and this does not necessarily have to be limited to *Jesus* or *Yeshua*. In the fifth verse of the twenty-third Psalm, the Psalmist talks about the anointing of his head with oil. Throughout the Bible, there are stories of people being anointed. Moses anointed his brother Aaron as the first high priest of Israel (Exodus 30:22-30). Even Miriam, Moses' sister, must have been anointed by the Holy Spirit to be given the title "prophetess" (Exodus 15:20). Long before David was appointed as king over the Israelite people, *YHWH* told Samuel to anoint him (1 Samuel 16:12-13). In life, we find that, in many cases, we are anointed before we are given the appointment or the assignment. Even after David's anointing, he returned to tending sheep before ascending to the throne.

We should endeavor to approach reading the Bible with a fresh anointing. Shifting our perspective on how we engage with the Bible does not alter the text itself; instead, it helps us to appreciate the fullness, richness, depth, and breadth of the bestselling book of all time. Another goal of this book is to level the playing field regarding understanding the Bible and its teachings, moving beyond white hegemonic interpretations and doctrine. Misinterpretations of biblical scripture have served as the catalyst for marital discord, family feuds, racial unrest, church splits, and even civil and global wars.

One of my hopes is that this book will also serve as a tool to teach white, Eurocentric individuals how to appreciate, or at least acknowledge, that some are reading the Bible from a non-white, non-European perspective. The Bible holds profound significance, especially for African Americans, serving as a source of spiritual nourishment and a tool for liberation. However, the interpretation of scripture has often been shaped by the dominant hegemonic cultural and theological frameworks that exclude the unique experiences and perspectives of the Afrodiasporic community. For members of the Afrodiaspora to fully engage with the Bible and its teachings, it is crucial to read it from an Afrodiasporic perspective—one that acknowledges the rich heritage, struggles, and aspirations of the entire culture.

Another hope I have for those who read, use, or study this book is to shift from the confines of religious rigidity to finding comfort in embracing spiritual fluidity, understanding that Christian soteriology or salvation is not as much about individual destiny as it is a communal lifelong quest.

Another aim of this book is to serve as a guide for reading and studying the Bible through three theological lenses: Black Liberation, Womanist, and Black Queer theologies—representing three subsets of the Afrodiasporic population. I emphasize the importance of avoiding what I call "church sign theology," which limits theological understanding to the brevity of a church sign or tweet. Such limitations risk hindering engagement on a spiritual or intellectual level necessary for spiritual transformation and growth.

Though I must acknowledge that I am not a subject matter expert on Womanist or Black Queer theologies, I intend to provide a sufficient introduction to enable readers to make rational and informed decisions when studying biblical scripture. These theologies operate on the fringes of society—in the Hush Harbors. I have grouped them under a broader category I like to refer to as Theologies of Righteous Indignation. I may follow up this book with my thoughts on Theologies of Righteous Indignation. Contumacious or stubborn believers often align somewhere within the spectrum of the Theology of Righteous Indignation. These three theological frameworks offer distinct perspectives that highlight marginalized voices, experiences, and liberating potential within the biblical text, challenging norms and expectations. At this juncture, these frameworks disrupt the waters of Western Christianity.

I hope this book and its content will open avenues for white European descendants to reconsider the Bible from a newer, more inclusive perspective. In the United States, evangelicalism often discourages intellectualism or critical readings of the Bible, particularly those originating from the fringes of the population. This discouragement stems from the misguided notion that questioning the Bible is equivalent to questioning *YHWH*. It is never a matter of choosing between the intellectual and spiritual reading of the Bible. When approaching sacred scripture, we must be ready to engage both the head and the heart. There is an awareness that should be present when we read the Bible.

Indeed, misguided teaching and preaching can distort the intended message of the Bible for individuals or specific groups. One person's understanding and interpretation of the Bible should not automatically negate another's. It is often okay to "agree to disagree" and move on instead of staunchly defending misunderstandings or misinterpretations, potentially alienating friends and family.

The eleventh chapter of the Book of Hebrews provides an excellent summary of the concept of faith. In the first verse, the writer describes faith as "the substance of things hoped for, the evidence of things not seen." (NIV) I take this to mean that even though we read scripture in the Bible or any other sacred canon of scripture, it's entirely plausible that our understanding today may be vastly different from our understanding a decade ago or what it might be a decade from now. The verse in Hebrews, referring to the evidence of things not seen, suggests that we can perceive insights in our minds' eyes as we read from the Bible.

Regardless of what we might think, the Bible was not directly dictated to its authors by *YHWH*; instead, the oral scrolls of the books of the Bible were divinely inspired.

Most importantly, the Bible is not *YHWH*. The power and the sacredness of scripture lie in how we interpret what we read and live our lives in relation to *YHWH*, our fellow human beings, and the rest of Creation. The intention is not to create better readers for the purpose of teaching Bible Study or Sunday School but rather to liberate individuals who may feel enslaved by a doctrinal and dogmatic reading of scripture.

Another key takeaway I hope readers gain from this book is removing any feeling of inadequacy resulting from comparisons with others in their faith circles who may have an unmatched memory recall of scripture. Being able to recite scripture on demand is akin to a mother bird regurgitating partially digested food to feed her hatchlings. The mother bird does not receive the complete nutrients from her food because some are given to the hatchlings.

The goal of the Gospels is not only to teach us how to live but also how to treat each other. Before starting seminary, people would say to me, "You better be deeply rooted in your faith when you go to seminary." Many of my fellow seminarians chose not to modify their thinking and understanding of the Bible and their faith. As a result, they graduated unchanged from who they were—their thoughts and understanding of Christianity and the Bible remained the same as before seminary.

Another critical point is understanding who we are as we engage with our faith. This principle extends beyond Christianity; it is inherent in humanism. In my personal exploration of Buddhist practice, one significant takeaway has been the liberation of the mind to embrace our sentience and the sentience of the entire Creation—the rich tapestry of flora and fauna. In Christianity, the aim is to find the path of enlightenment that enables us to be who we are called or created to be. Developing an awareness of one's identity while reading the Bible is more important than one may think. No one reads anything devoid of their personal context, which is especially true for reading scripture. Reading the Bible should be seen as only a part of a holistic approach to one's faith journey.

One disservice cradle-to-grave Christians do to new believers is responding to their personal problems with a common instinct: "Pray about it and read your Bible." However, for most Christians, regardless of their experience, prayer and Bible reading are not innate or natural to our being. The Western mainstream church fails to equip its members with a complete understanding of the significance of these practices for both individuals and the community of believers.

Another goal of this book is to serve as a basic introduction to reading a book that continues to baffle modern-day scholars and theologians. Reading the Bible should not be treated like reading a storybook, school textbook, or self-help book. The Bible narrates the history of a specific group of people during a particular time in a certain region of the world, outlining their relationship with their God, their Creator.

Additionally, this book aims to liberate long-term Christians from the dangers of bibliolatry, literalization, and weaponization.

Bibliolatry is just what it sounds like, the reverence and idolization of the Bible to the detriment of understanding its true importance.[7] It is the root cause of the literalization and weaponization of scripture. By literalization, I am describing how Bible readers treat the text as timeless, as the actual spoken Word of *YHWH*, not to be questioned. People use the logical fallacy of circular reasoning to validate the Bible using the Bible.

Like literalization, the reader's interpretation is foundational to weaponization. Weaponizing scripture occurs when one uses biblical scripture to justify the mistreatment of others, including enslavement or genocide. Bible verses have been used to justify war, violent invasions, and the colonization of indigenous lands globally. When the Bible is used to abuse others and deny their humanity/divinity, it is not reading; it is "cherry-picking" scripture out of its context.

I must admit to being guilty of proof-texting the Bible, the act of finding scripture to fit a particular situation or ideology, even if it means taking the text out of context. It is easy to conceive an idea or concept, search commentaries or the internet for scripture that seemingly supports it, and create a sermon without thorough exegesis or consideration of the text's social, historical, political, or theological context. The danger is that taking scripture out of context for the sake of creating a sermon is akin to creating a con; as the saying goes among theologians, preachers, and biblical scholars: "When you take the *text* out of *context*, all you are left with is a *con*."

Reading scripture as a faith practice is not the same as reading a book for academic purposes; it is more about engaging with the text, not just reading Bible stories to pass some "Christian test" or to complete a mythological quest. Engaging with the text combines hermeneutics and exegesis; tools preachers have used for years. Biblical reading for faith practice is not superficial; engagement with scripture must be deliberate and intentional.

A part of engaging scripture is understanding your social location. This understanding represents one of the most critical components of reading scripture. What is meant by social location? It encompasses the entirety of who you are as a person. Your social location is the holistic sum of factors such as "gender, race, social class, age, ability, religion, sexual orientation, and geographic location."[8] No two individuals share the same social location; it is as unique as a fingerprint.

The primary objective of this book is to empower readers to engage with the Bible from an African American perspective, incorporating the transformative insights offered by Black Liberation, Womanist, and Black Queer Theologies. By doing so, we aim to deepen our understanding of the biblical text, reclaim our spiritual heritage, and find inspiration and guidance for our personal and collective journeys.

In pursuit of these objectives, this book is structured as follows:

Chapter 1: Understanding the White Gaze and the Black Existential Fight to Be

Chapter 2: Is the Bible Holy?

Chapter 3: Understanding African American Biblical Interpretation

Chapter 4: Black Liberation Theology and the Bible

Chapter 5: Womanist Theology and the Bible: A Black Man's Perspective

Chapter 6: Black Queer Theology and the Bible: A Heteronormative Black Man's Perspective

Chapter 7: Integrating Perspectives: Reading the Bible Holistically

Chapter 8: Application and Praxis

Chapters 4-6 delve into each theological framework's foundational principles, key concepts, and biblical insights. I will explore relevant scriptures, engage with scholarly perspectives, and provide practical guidance for incorporating these perspectives into our reading and interpretation of the Bible. Furthermore, I will examine the implications of an African American perspective on ethical considerations, community engagement, and personal spiritual practice.

By the end of this book, I hope readers will be equipped with the knowledge, tools, and inspiration to read the Bible from an Afrodiasporic perspective. Such an approach will deepen our understanding of scripture and empower us to live out our faith in ways that promote justice, liberation, and love in our communities. Together, we shall embark on a transformative journey, discovering the richness of the Bible through the Afrodiasporic lens and embracing the liberating possibilities it holds for us and our world.

[1] Allison Task, "What Is Ubuntu Philosophy & What Can We Learn From It? - Allison Task," February 23, 2023, https://allisontask.com/ubuntu-philosophy/.

[2] "What We Can Learn from the African Philosophy of Ubuntu - BBC REEL - YouTube," accessed August 31, 2023, https://www.youtube.com/.

[3] Frank A. Thomas, *Introduction to the Practice of African American Preaching* (Nashville: Abingdon Press, 2016), 8.

[4] David F. Ford, ed., *The Modern Theologians: An Introduction to Christian Theology in the Twentieth Century*, Second edition, The Great Theologians (Cambridge, Mass: Blackwell, 1997).

[5] David Polk, "Toni Morrison On Writing Without the 'White Gaze' | American Masters | PBS," American Masters, June 18, 2020, https://www.pbs.org/wnet/americanmasters/toni-morrison-on-writing-without-the-white-gaze/14874/.

[6] *Our African Unconscious*, 2021, xv.-xvii., https://www.simonandschuster.com/books/Our-African-Unconscious/Edward-Bruce-Bynum/9781644113967.

[7] *Pocket Dictionary of Biblical Studies: Over 300 Terms Clearly & Concisely Defined*, 21, accessed August 26, 2022, https://www.christianbook.com/dictionary-biblical-studies-clearly-concisely-defined/arthur-patzia/9780830814671/pd/14674.

[8] "Inclusion and Diversity Committee Report: What's Your Social Location?," National Council on Family Relations, accessed August 24, 2022, https://www.ncfr.org/ncfr-report/spring-2019/inclusion-and-diversity-social-location.

CHAPTER TWO

Understanding the White Gaze and the Black Existential Fight to Be

***

"It took many years of vomiting up all the filth I'd been taught about myself, and half-believed, before I was able to walk on the earth as though I had a right to be here."
-James Baldwin[1]

***

"I'm just a nobody trying to tell everybody about somebody, who can save anybody."
-The Williams Brothers[2]

***

In an interview, Toni Morrison discusses the criticism she received for not writing for a broader (i.e., whiter) audience. Critics attacked her work for its absence of white characters, seemingly overlooking that Irish-Americans, French-Americans, Dutch-Americans, and other hyphenated white European American writers rarely receive the same scrutiny. The White Gaze shapes how we perceive life and interact with all media types, be it music, audio recordings, books, artwork, or video.[3] There is a thought that the victor determines the narrative's direction and decides whether the narrative exists at all. In the context of the United States, whiteness stands as the victor, having historically and currently shaped the American narrative.

The Bible is a unique narrative with a global reach. Interestingly, it tells the story of the relationship between a specific group of people and their Creator. However, this narrative has often fallen victim to cultural appropriation. Before the fourteenth century, the Bible was intended exclusively for reading and interpretation by the church clergy. Interestingly, people from so many different cultures can read the story of Pharaoh enslaving the Israelites, with all of them assuming the role of the enslaved rather than that of Pharaoh and the Egyptians.

Throughout history, I have yet to see any people, especially those in power admit to being Pharaoh—responsible for the mistreatment of others simply because "they could, so they did." The Afrodiaspora in the United States has endured Pharaoh's knee on their necks for four centuries and counting. No other group of people has endured centuries of suffering and trauma at the hands of European peoples around the world.

It was not until seminary that I learned about the White Gaze and its pervasiveness. During an Old Testament class, I discovered how people of different ethnicities read the biblical text.

A prime example was the story of Abraham, Sarah, and their slave, Hagar. I've learned that white Christians see the story through a completely different lens—through the lens of the White Gaze. Hagar, the slave, is seen as being disobedient and disrespectful to Sarah. However, Black readers typically see her as the victim of Sarah and Abraham's scheme to do what they did not trust *YHWH* to do.

The "othering" of Hagar has even made its way into Black evangelical theological understanding. The goal of the White Gaze is the worship of whiteness by proxy. For the longest time, the vision of Christianity in the United States was synonymous with churches featuring stained glass windows adorned with the iconography of white European men. The Creator became the created, seen in the image of the hegemony.

I remember growing up and visiting different Black churches in my community and seeing similar images of the bearded "Santa-esque" white man in a white robe with long flowing white hair—often displayed in framed paintings or murals on the wall. In these churches, the image of the white Christ was prominent. The Black Church Trinity usually comprised Martin Luther King, Jr., John F. Kennedy, and the blond-haired, blue-eyed Christ. These images, especially that of Christ, made it hard for many Black Christians to see themselves as being worthy of Jesus' love.

There is a stark difference between Jesus and "the Christ." Images of "the Christ" represent a spiritual overseer, limiting the move of the Holy Spirit among the Afrodiaspora. Jesus was the personal Savior of Black people; He was the One to whom our ancestors could speak directly and who answered their cries and prayers. Our ancestors found Jesus, sang to Him, prayed to Him, and worshipped with Him at the Hush Harbors.

Until 2017, the National Cathedral in our nation's capital had stained glass windows with images of the Confederacy, installed in the mid-twentieth century. The conversation about removing the windows only started in 2015 with the mass shooting at Emanuel AME Church in Charleston, SC. However, no action was taken until the Unite the Right Rally in 2017 in Charlottesville, VA.[4]

Imagine, almost one century after the end of the Civil War, a church in the nation's capital thought it would be okay to install imagery honoring the Confederacy. This is a church whose claim is that it is "[g]rounded in the reconciling love of Jesus Christ" and that it "is a house of prayer for all people, conceived by our founders to serve as a great church for national purposes." For all people, really?! For nearly a century, the leadership of the second-largest cathedral in the United States never thought twice or never cared about the moral and spiritual damage the Confederate imagery might inflict on its Afrodiasporan worshippers, which included the first Black President of the United States, Barack Obama, and his family.

The National Cathedral is but a microcosm of the failure of the hegemony to empathize with the lives of others who do not look like them.

The Afrodiaspora is a group of people whose culture intersects with Biblical scripture. Members of the Afrodiaspora have learned the process of deconstructing the teachings of the Bible, which historically advocated for subservience and obedience to their masters while simultaneously striving to reclaim their very essence. We have had to learn what it meant to seek freedom while seemingly trapped in a perpetual state of enslavement. Even after slavery was outlawed in the United States, the challenge shifted to preserving the identity marked by "Blackness." The transition from enslavement to freedom wasn't immediate for African peoples. The U.S. Negro status of "nothingness" became real through an "ontometaphysical holocaust."[5]

I would like to close out this chapter with a song by one of my favorite artists, Nina Simone—"I Wish I Knew How It Would Feel to Be Free" (October 1967):

I wish I knew how it would feel to be free
I wish I could break all the chains holding me
I wish I could say all the things that I should say
Say 'em loud, say 'em clear
For the whole round world to hear

I wish I could share all the love that's in my heart
Remove all the bars that keep us apart
I wish you could know what it means to be me
Then you'd see and agree
That every man should be free
I wish I could give all I'm longing to give
I wish I could live like I'm longing to live
I wish I could do all the things that I can do
Though I'm way overdue, I'd be starting anew

Well, I wish I could be like a bird in the sky
How sweet it would be if I found I could fly
Oh, I'd soar to the sun and look down at the sea
And then I'd sing 'cause I'd know, yeah
Then I'd sing 'cause I'd know, yeah
Then I'd sing 'cause I'd know
I'd know how it feels
I'd know how it feels to be free, yeah, yeah
Oh, I'd know how it feels
Yes, I'd know, I'd know how it feels
How it feels to be free, Lord, Lord, Lord, yeah

I'd know how it feels
I'd know how it feels to be free, yeah, yeah
Oh, I'd know how it feels
Yes, I'd know, I'd know how it feels
How it feels to be free, Lord, Lord, Lord, yeah[6]

[1] Helios Publishing, *James Baldwin's Little Book of Selected Quotes*, n.d., 6.

[2] "I'm Just a Nobody Lyrics - Google Search," accessed September 1, 2023, https://www.google.com/search?client=safari&rls=en&q=i%27m+just+a+nobody+lyrics&ie=UTF-8&oe=UTF-8.

[3] David Polk, "Toni Morrison On Writing Without the 'White Gaze' | American Masters | PBS," American Masters, June 18, 2020, https://www.pbs.org/wnet/americanmasters/toni-morrison-on-writing-without-the-white-gaze/14874/.

[4] "National Cathedral's Confederate-Themed Stained Glass to Be Replaced with Racial Justice Imagery to 'Tell the Truth' of Country's Past - CBS News," September

24, 2021, https://www.cbsnews.com/news/national-cathedral-confederate-stained-glass-replaced-racial-justice-imagery/.

[5] Calvin L. Warren, *Ontological Terror: Blackness, Nihilism, and Emancipation* (Durham, NC: Duke University Press, 2018), loc. 622 of 5464.

[6] *Nina Simone – I Wish I Knew How It Would Feel To Be Free*, accessed December 6, 2023, https://genius.com/Nina-simone-i-wish-i-knew-how-it-would-feel-to-be-free-lyrics.

CHAPTER THREE

Understanding African American Biblical Interpretation

***

"We call on your protection — from spaces that do not always apprehend the image of God in us, from systems that do not uphold our dignity."
-Cole Arthur Riley[1]

***

Is the Bible Holy?

The Bible is not sacred! The Bible is not holy! There, I said it! Please hear me out before you tear up this book and toss it into your fireplace or fire pit. I hope to redeem myself concerning the respect due to the canon of scripture we call the Bible.

The Bible, on its own, is not inherently sacred or holy. It possesses no inherent power; holding a paper Bible in one's hand or keeping one in your car's back window does not make you more of a Christian than someone who carries the Bible app on their smartphone, just as sitting in a garage does not make you a car.

Some of you may think I am going to hell with gasoline drawers on. Please do not stop reading because I assure you that I do believe in the Bible and its proper role in the Christian faith. However, I also believe that for too long, Western Christians have treated the Bible with the same level of reverence as *YHWH*.

Many Western Christians treat the Bible as the magic bottle that contains the "Genie," who appears when you open the book and grant your wishes if you recite the right verses and pray the right incantation. While we can find *YHWH* within the pages of scripture, everything there is to know about *YHWH* cannot possibly be confined to the potpourri of divinely inspired writings we call the Bible. It is even written at the conclusion of the New Testament Gospel of John that the Bible does not contain all there is to know about Yeshua (John 21:25).

If the Bible is acknowledged as not containing all there is to know about the life of Yeshua, how can we expect it to have all there is to know about life, especially twenty-first-century life? So, for those of you who believe in the sanctity of Trinitarian doctrine, you should also question what we might think we know about *YHWH*.

Many people feel that they can read and understand the thoughts of a Supreme Being and the guidance intended for each of us. When reading the Bible, one finds that its contents span from the sacred to the secular, even into the profane, and then back into the secular and the sacred. Many preachers avoid the Bible's darker or more challenging aspects, perhaps out of fear of being unable to redeem these writings and continue to provide the people with hope.

Hermeneutics

What are hermeneutics? Do you need a seminary degree to understand it? Answering the second question first: no, you do not have to have a seminary degree or any degree for that matter to apply hermeneutics. Hermeneutics is not restricted to religious texts or scriptures.

However, for the purposes of this book, when referring to hermeneutics, we will limit the discussion to the field of biblical hermeneutics. Unbeknownst to many, we employ hermeneutics when reading the Bible, though we may not be aware of our specific method. Hermeneutics is the art and science of interpretation, emphasizing the "how" of interpreting the Bible. [2]

Social Location

What is your social location? The better basic question might be, "What is social location?" Social location is what makes us who we are, the intersection of "gender, race, social class, age, ability, religion, sexual orientation, and geographic location."[3]Understanding your social location might help you better understand why you believe what you believe when you engage with scripture. It helps people understand that no one reads the Bible, irrespective of who they are.

If you are a Black middle-class woman raised in the South in the sixties, you will read the Bible scripture differently from a white male farmer raised in the Midwest in the sixties or even a Black middle-class man raised in the South in the sixties. Your social location shapes your theology but does not confine you to a specific theology. As a Black woman, you may have an affinity for feminist or womanist theology. As a white man, your theology may have the characteristics of a white cisgender, patriarchal Eurocentric theology. As a Latinx individual living in the United States, Liberation or Mujerista theology may influence your Christian faith.

The beauty of scripture is its ability to speak to us across social locations. Even within our own social locations, as we age or as our social location changes, we may read scripture with a different understanding than when we started reading the Bible.

Reading is Fundamental

There are 26 letters in the English alphabet. Most children in the United States learn the letters via song and word association—"A is for apple, B is for ball..." More contemporary educational videos, like Gracie's Corner, use hip beats and rhythmic lyrics to get and keep children's attention. So, even before we learn to spell words, we use word associations to familiarize ourselves with the alphabet. Through this process, we give meaning to the symbols we call letters.

One problem with word association is that speaking English doesn't guarantee understanding every word in the language, which constantly evolves. Today's dictionaries include words that may not have existed when some of us learned grammar in the mid to late twentieth century. I recall growing up when the word "ain't" was not in the dictionary. In some school contexts, its use in writing was even forbidden.

Another issue with word association arises when describing something unfamiliar, a challenge often emphasized in the context of standardized testing for students of color or impoverished children.

Reading is essential, providing access to knowledge, facts, and more. Over a one-year period, 1,621 people were surveyed, and nearly 50% of the respondents had not read a book in over a year. The same study also highlighted the percentage of non-readers increasing with age. Another consideration is the mechanics of reading. I will first address reading comprehension.

Reading comprehension is introduced to many individuals as early as the third grade. The third-grade reading level is a standard measure of future educational achievement in the United States. It is also a statistic used by those in control of the Prison Industrial Complex (PIC) to determine future prison populations. If a person finishes the third grade and is below the standard reading level for their age, it may indicate future reading and comprehension issues. Reading comprehension is the ability to understand what one reads. For students taking standardized tests, including college entrance exams, reading comprehension is a metric to determine future success in school and life. On tests, reading comprehension is reading a paragraph or passage and answering subsequent questions to determine if the reader understood what they just read.

When I was growing up, the nonprofit organization Reading is Fundamental led a children's literacy campaign. The organization's basis for existence was to use literacy to aid social justice and equity. Reading is fundamental to many things. If there is one thing that cannot be taken for granted in our education system, reading is one of the core competencies that form the foundation of everything else we learn. While many think math and science are exempt, math requires reading problems, and science requires reading theories and formulas.

As social media has become the preeminent communication medium, emojis and abbreviations of phrases (or acronyms) have become commonplace. LOL (Laughing Out Loud), ROTFL (Rolling On The Floor Laughing), and TTYL (Talk To You Later) have become societal standards for communicating via text or social media posts and comments, even being read as words themselves. As this textspeak or chatspeak has become more popular, I sincerely believe that reading levels are dropping, and we have all but lost the ability to read and read critically.

In addition, the legislation and pushback from Republican government officials against "Woke Culture" and any form of intellectualism contribute to a lack of critical reading. So, what is critical reading? Terry Heick writes, "[c]ritical reading is reading with the purpose of critical examination of the text and its implicit and explicit themes and ideas."[4] As you will see later, critical reading is of utmost importance when reading biblical scripture as it enables engagement with the text.

So, what is the cause of our misinterpretations and mistranslations of the Bible? One of the most important things I learned in the U.S. Naval Submarine Force is that there is a reason for everything, whether good or bad. After a casualty or an incident onboard a nuclear submarine, we had procedures to assign a senior enlisted person or an officer to investigate. When the Navy conducts internal investigations of casualties or incidents, the reasons for what happened are always narrowed down to three categories. The first category is that of the individual or the operator. The second category is the equipment, and the final category is issues with the written procedure. Everything that could have gone wrong and did go wrong fits into one of those three categories. Our misunderstandings and mistranslations of sacred scripture fit into one of three categories.

The first category of errant biblical translation or misinterpretation is our misunderstanding or mistranslation of the Bible, which is the root cause of operator error. The second category is the poor translation of the biblical translation we read. This falls under the root cause of equipment failure.

The King James Version (KJV) is not one of the most reader-friendly translations but one of the most widely used translations in mainstream Western evangelical Christianity. It has a sordid origin story and is written at a 12th-grade reading level, while the average American reads at an 8th-grade level. Only some biblical translations remain faithful to the original languages.

Why is this important? About 14% of Americans are functionally illiterate, while nearly 50% of Americans need help to read at an 8th-grade reading level. These numbers are even worse for the Afrodiasporan population.[5]

Again, why is this important? Our churches, especially in the "Bible Belt," tend to be filled with people with poor reading skills. In the South, it is not uncommon to find many people in the pews, even in the pulpits, who cannot read at an 8th-grade level. The bigger problem goes beyond reading ability to the ability to comprehend what you read. I am not equating a person's faith with their ability to read, but there must be some consideration as to whether people understand the texts from which we preach and teach enough to conduct fruitful independent study.

The final category is the study process we learned, even though there has yet to be a written procedure for many of us. As we read through scripture, we must consider our understanding or translation as not the final or only understanding or translation. For as many people that claim, "the Bible says it, and that's it," we are making claims that are not without issue. This book aims to help Western Christians, specifically the Afrodiaspora, understand there must be a perspective change, a paradigm shift. In that shift, we must accept that we do not have it all figured out and might even have it wrong.

Biblical Literacy

Literacy has been addressed. It is essential that we make the distinction between general literacy and biblical literacy. The Bible complicates the issue with transliterations and multiple translations from ancient languages written by groups of people, which is derived from an extensive oral history.

Below is a list of the reading levels of various translations of the Bible.[6]

- King James Version (KJV) — 12
- Revised Standard Version (RSV) — 12
- New Revised Standard Version (NRSV) — 11
- New American Standard Bible (NASB) — 11
- English Standard Version (ESV) — 10
- Holman Christian Standard Bible (HCSB) — 7-8
- New International Version (NIV) — 7-8
- Common English Bible (CEB) — 7
- Christian Standard Bible (CSB) — 7
- New King James Version (NKJV) — 7
- New Living Translation (NLT) — 6
- God's Word (GW) — 5
- Message — 4-5
- New Century Version (NCV) — 3
- New International Reader's Version (NIrV) — 3

As you can see from the above list, the reading level of the KJV is the highest, especially relative to more recent translations. The average literacy rate across the nation is 88%. That means an average of 12 out of 100 are illiterate. When I was stationed in Charleston, SC, from 2005-2007, I was a volunteer tutor for a literacy program for firefighters. Many of Charleston's Black firefighters were unable to read street signs and had been grandfathered in to remain employed, with future plans for the department to provide literacy training.

At the root of biblical literalism is biblical fundamentalism, and ignorance is the root of biblical fundamentalism. There are too many Western Christians who believe the Israelites are *YHWH*'s chosen people while also believing the current Jewish people who do not accept Jesus as their LORD and Savior. Because of this, Western Christians' belief system is ineffectual. For example, the Resurrection of Jesus is seen as more of a physical event, as merely a physical resuscitation. Biblical stories are much more than they appear to be at face value.[7] What is the best translation of the Bible to read? My answer is simple: the one that you can read and understand.

Preparation for Reading the Bible

Just as professional athletes have pre-game routines, it is critical to develop a pre-reading routine when it comes to reading the Bible. This is not to say that the Bible cannot be read for pleasure but to unlock the true power of the Bible; one must put oneself in a particular mindset. Picking up a Bible and reading it when one is sad, depressed, or angry may not yield the expected results.

Another thing that makes reading the Bible harder is the apparent cognitive dissonance between the actions of your faith community and what you understand from reading the Bible. In many cases, it is a battle between doctrine and dogma that does not align with biblical teachings.

The first preparation step is all about emptying. As much as possible, one must empty oneself of doctrinal or dogmatic thinking when reading the Bible. One must also rid oneself of feelings of inadequacy and low self-esteem. A reader must never silence their own inner voice and should honor their intersectionality, their whole self. Another recommendation is not to anticipate your previous interpretation and understanding of scripture as the "final answer." The reader should embrace a state of mindfulness or self-awareness. Mindfulness is being aware of your current emotions, circumstances, and where you are on your spiritual journey.[8]

The second preparation step is to think theologically when reading biblical scripture. This can be a challenging process because one of the components of reading the Bible theologically is the use of intellect. In other words, it is imperative to feel liberated enough to honor your understanding of what you are reading but also liberated enough to realize you may not fully comprehend what you just read, and that is alright.

Overview of African American Biblical Interpretation as a Distinct Theological Tradition

Afrodiasporic biblical interpretation is a vibrant theological tradition that arose from the African Diaspora's unique experiences and struggles in the United States. It is the response to the call of the historical and social context shaping the Afrodiasporan engagement with the Bible. This distinct theological tradition offers valuable insights into scripture and provides a lens through which the African Diaspora can reclaim their spiritual heritage and find empowerment and liberation.

African American biblical interpretation draws upon Black Liberation, Womanist, and Black Queer theological frameworks to engage with the biblical text in ways that reflect the totality of African Diasporan experiences, aspirations, and challenges. These frameworks have significantly shaped the Afrodiasporic understanding of scripture, offering alternative readings and interpretations that challenge dominant narratives and bring marginalized voices to the forefront.

Historical and Social Context of Afrodiasporic Engagement with the Bible

To truly grasp the significance of Afrodiasporan biblical interpretation, we must explore the historical and social context from which it emerged. From the days of slavery to the present day, the African Diaspora has turned to the Bible as a source of strength, hope, and resistance. The Bible provided solace and inspiration during times of oppression, serving as a guide for navigating the complexities of life and a source of liberation theology.

During slavery, the African peoples were exposed to white Euro-centric biblical teachings of Christianity tailored for oppression and enslavement. However, they found ways to reinterpret and internalize the biblical message in ways that affirmed their humanity, resilience, and desire for freedom. They identified with biblical figures such as Moses, who led the Israelites out of bondage, and Jesus, who stood in solidarity with the marginalized and oppressed.

Following emancipation, the Afrodiaspora established churches and developed theological perspectives addressing their unique experiences. These perspectives became the foundation for Afrodiasporan biblical interpretation, laying the groundwork for the emergence of Black Liberation, Womanist, and Black Queer Theologies. These theologies are part of an ever-growing category of theologies I call Theologies of Righteous Indignation.

Why Righteous Indignation, you might ask? Righteous Indignation is not simply a matter of anger but anger shrouded in contempt. This may be akin to what Berlinerblau calls "counterexegesis" or reading against the text. It is not just a matter of being opposed to the text. In other words, it is as if we are in a sailboat, and our chosen direction of motion happens to be into the wind, which requires some navigational skill and knowledge.[9] Of the three, Black Queer Theology does the best job of disregarding normative readings of scripture.

Significance of Black Liberation, Womanist, and Black Queer Theologies in African American Biblical Interpretation

Black Liberation, Womanist, and Black Queer theologies signifi-cantly influence African American biblical interpretation, expanding the theological landscape and providing alternative perspectives on scripture. These frameworks give voice to the marginalized, challenge oppressive systems, and promote liberation and justice.

Black Liberation Theology, deeply rooted in the Afrodiasporan struggle for freedom and justice, reshapes the Afrodiasporan understanding of the Bible. It highlights themes of liberation, solidarity, and resistance within scripture, challenging oppressive systems and calling for social transformation. Black Liberation Theology empowers the African Diaspora to read the Bible, consider their own experiences, and provide a theological framework that inspires activism and the pursuit of justice.

Womanist Theology, rooted in the experiences and wisdom of Black women, centers their voices on biblical interpretation. It addresses Black women's unique challenges and provides a framework for understanding their agency, spirituality, and contributions within the Bible and society. Womanist Theology emphasizes the interconnectedness of race, gender, and class, shedding light on the experiences of Black women and offering a transformative perspective on scripture.

Black Queer Theology offers a lens through which the African Diaspora can explore the intersections of sexuality, gender, and identity within the Bible. It challenges heteronormative interpretations and highlights the inherent dignity and worth of every person, regardless of their sexual orientation or gender identity. Black Queer Theology disrupts dominant interpretations, opening new possibilities for inclusivity, love, and acceptance within the African Diasporan theological tradition.

This chapter laid the foundation for understanding Afrodiasporan biblical interpretation as a distinct theological tradition. I have explored the historical and social context that shaped Afrodiasporan engagement with the Bible and the significance of Black Liberation, Womanist, and Queer Theologies within this context. In the following chapters, we will delve deeper into these theological frameworks, examining their key principles, biblical insights, and practical implications for reading the Bible from an Afrodiasporan perspective. Through this exploration, I aim to equip readers with the tools and insights needed to engage with scripture in transformative ways, embracing the fullness of our Afrodiasporan identity and spirituality.

[1] Cole Arthur Riley, "God of the Black Woman," The Presbyterian Outlook, May 17, 2022, https://pres-outlook.org/2022/05/god-of-the-black-woman/.

[2] Andrew P. Rogers, *Congregational Hermeneutics: How Do We Read?* (London: Routledge, 2016), 6, https://doi.org/10.4324/9781315562995.

[3] "Inclusion and Diversity Committee Report: What's Your Social Location?," National Council on Family Relations, accessed August 24, 2022, https://www.ncfr.org/ncfr-report/spring-2019/inclusion-and-diversity-social-location.

[4] Terry Heick, "What Is Critical Reading? A Definition For Learning," TeachThought, March 8, 2022, https://www.teachthought.com/literacy/what-is-critical-readinYHWHefinition/.

[5] Irwin S Kirrsch et al., "Adult Literacy in America," n.d., 16–21.

[6] "Bible Translation Reading Levels - Christianbook.Com," accessed August 24, 2022, https://www.christianbook.com/page/bibles/about-bibles/bible-translation-reading-levels.

[7] John Shelby Spong, *Biblical Literalism: A Gentile Heresy: A Journey into a New Christianity through the Doorway of Matthew's Gospel*, First edition (San Francisco: HarperOne, an imprint of Harper Collins Publishers, 2016), 3–4.

[8] Eric D. Barreto, ed., *Thinking Theologically: Foundations for Learning*, Foundations for Learning (Minneapolis, MN: Fortress Press, 2015), 13–20.

[9] Teresa J. Hornsby and Ken Stone, *Bible Trouble: Queer Reading at the Boundaries of Biblical Scholarship* (Atlanta: Society of Biblical Literature, 2011), 3.

CHAPTER FOUR

Black Liberation Theology and the Bible

***

"To become Black is to experience an ontological catastrophe. It is to constantly struggle with the possibilities of human life in the midst of a dehumanizing reality."
-Nathalie Etoke[1]

***

I ask that you not consider the size of this chapter as an indication of the importance I place on it for the Afrodiaspora. If you google "Black Liberation Theology, you will see much more compared to that of Womanist and Black Queer theologies. Today's African Diaspora in the West was born through the tortuous birth canal of the Middle Passage, with over two centuries of the labor pains of kidnapping, captivity, torture, and enslavement. The call for reparations does not fall on deaf ears. The descendants of the enslavers and those who benefited from the free labor know that the restitution would be astronomical, bankrupting the corporations and possibly tripling or quadrupling the national debt.

Black Liberation Theology emerged in response to the systemic oppression faced by African Americans, addressing issues that Latino-based Liberation Theology did not cover. It emphasizes liberation, justice, and the pursuit of equality for the Afrodiaspora. Black Liberation

Theology recognizes the Bible as a tool of empowerment and liberation, challenging oppressive systems and calling for societal transformation. It highlights biblical themes of freedom, solidarity, and resistance, grounding African Diasporan faith in the struggle for justice. True Black Liberation Theology is not limited to the constraints of the Christian religion. The Afrodiaspora are members of various world religions.

Black Liberation Theology emerged as a robust theological framework in the mid-20th century, giving voice to African Americans' experiences, struggles, and aspirations. It sought to address the systemic oppression faced by Black communities and offer a liberating interpretation of the Bible that resonates with our collective journey to freedom and equality. In this chapter, we will explore the profound impact of Black Liberation Theology on Afrodiasporan biblical interpretation.

The Theological and Sociopolitical Foundations of Black Liberation Theology

Black Liberation Theology believes *YHWH* stands with the oppressed and marginalized, actively working for the liberation of and justice for the African Diaspora. It emerged in response to claims by Black Muslims, Black secular Marxists, Pan-Africanists, and Black Nationalists that Christianity was a white man's religion.[2] Black Liberation Theology challenges traditional theological frameworks that uphold oppressive systems and center the interests of dominant groups. It seeks to dismantle racism, economic inequality, and other forms of injustice through the lens of scripture and the teachings of Jesus Christ. If the moral arc of the universe bends toward justice, Black Liberation Theology is the motive force that bends the arc.

Drawing inspiration from the Civil Rights Movement, the Black Power Movement, and the broader struggle for social and political liberation, Black Liberation Theology recognizes the interconnectedness of faith and activism. It emphasizes the importance of collective liberation, recognizing that true freedom can only be achieved when all members of society are liberated.

Black Liberation Theology invites the African Diaspora to critically examine biblical texts, focusing on themes of liberation, justice, and solidarity to serve as the roadmap for the Beloved Community. By centering the experiences of the oppressed and marginalized, it sheds light on the liberating messages embedded within the biblical narrative.

Key biblical stories such as the Exodus, where the Israelites were freed from bondage, take on profound significance within Black Liberation Theology. This liberation story resonates deeply with the Afrodiasporan experiences of slavery and ongoing struggles against racial injustice. Notably, one of the Bibles I own is called the *Slave Bible*. In this Bible, the originators decided it would be to their advantage not to include any scripture depicting liberation. That is why this particular Bible has nothing about the story of the Exodus of the people of Israel. This was the Bible our ancestors were allowed to possess, read, or be preached to.

As we move to the New Testament, the teachings of Jesus, who stood in solidarity with the marginalized and challenged oppressive systems, are seen as a call to action for social transformation.

The visionary leadership and activism of numerous Black scholars, theologians, and activists have shaped black Liberation Theology. James Cone, often regarded as the father of Black Liberation Theology, played a pivotal role in its development. His groundbreaking works, such as *A Black Theology of Liberation, Black Theology and Black Power, God of the Oppressed, and The Cross and the Lynching Tree,* provide a theological foundation for Black Liberation Theology.

Other influential figures in Black Liberation Theology include Dr. Jacqueline Grant, Dr. Cornel West, and Dr. Katie Cannon, among many others. Their scholarship, activism, and theological insights have contributed to a robust understanding of liberation and justice within the biblical interpretation of the African Diaspora.

Contemporary scholars and theologians continue to build upon the foundations laid by their predecessors. Their work expands the discourse on Black Liberation Theology, applying its principles to address pressing issues of our time, such as mass incarceration, police brutality, and economic inequality. These scholars, such as Drs. J. Kameron Carter, Kelly Brown Douglas, Mitzi Smith, Wil Gafney, Thomas Slater, Dwight N. Hopkins, Andre Johnson, and William Pinn offer fresh perspectives and further the ongoing development of Black Liberation Theology.

[1] Nathalie Etoke, *Black Existential Freedom*, Living Existentialism (Lanham: Rowman & Littlefield Publishers, 2023), loc. 36 of 221.

[2] James H. Evans, *We Have Been Believers: An Afrodiasporan Systematic Theology* (Minneapolis: Fortress Press, 1992), 4.

CHAPTER FIVE

Womanist Theology and the Bible: A Black Man's Perspective

***

"This is a man's world, but it wouldn't be nothing, nothing without a woman or a girl."[1]
-James Brown

***

"The failure of the Black church and Black theology to proclaim explicitly the liberation of Black women indicates that they cannot claim to be agents of divine liberation. If the theology, like the church, has no word for Black women, its conception of liberation is inauthentic."
-Jacquelyn Grant[2]

***

I can hear some of you now: What does a Black heteronormative man know about the plight of the Black Woman? My answer is not any more than I have been witness to throughout my life. Because I have chosen to allow my life as a Black man to intersect with that of the Black woman, I submit that womanism informs my empathy and compassion for all of humanity. Womanist Theology, forged within the wombs of Black women's experiences, centers the voices and perspectives of

Black women in biblical interpretation. It explores the intersections of race, gender, and class, acknowledging Black women's unique struggles and resilience. Womanist Theology offers valuable insights into biblical narratives, revealing Black women's agency, wisdom, and spirituality within the text.

Womanist Theology emerged in the late 20th century as a response to the limitations of traditional theological frameworks that failed to address Black women's unique experiences and perspectives.[3] It is rooted in the rich history of Afrodiasporan women's spiritual traditions, resistance movements, and cultural expressions. Womanist Theology recognizes the interconnectedness of race, gender, and class and seeks to liberate and empower Black women in their engagement with the Bible.

Black women battle on multiple fronts, specifically those of racism, sexism, and classism. It is at the intersectionality of their existence that we find the Black woman who, in many cases, is only allowed to occupy one status at a time because allowing otherwise would be an admission by society of its systemic oppression of the Black woman. Either she is Black, or she is a woman; society will not allow her to inhabit both spaces simultaneously. Intersectionality is what allows the Black woman a metaphysical state of being.[4] As a fan of DC comics, I liken the Black woman's existence to that of the multiverse, multiple universes overlapping in time and space. The Black woman has been forced to be a human microcosm of the multiverse concept.

Black women are the most oppressed yet most resilient humans. This is not based on the "strong Black woman" trope. Afrodiasporan women are the fruits of Eve's motherhood, the hope of Ruth, the strength of Deborah, the tenacity of Zelophehad's daughters, and the faith of Yeshua's mother, Mary.

Through Dr. Wil Gafney's commentary, I learned the importance of saying women's names in the Bible when provided. For example, in the 27th Chapter of Numbers, we come across a group of five sisters, the aforementioned Zelophehad's daughters, who have no problem challenging the status quo. In typical evangelical Christian settings, the story's characters are called "Zelophehad's daughters," as if they are nameless. Gafney demands we "say their names," that we see them, recognize their pivotal role in breaking societal norms, and give them the common courtesy of saying their names.

These women were well ahead of their time, even by today's standards. Mahlah, Noah, Hoglah, Milcah, and Tirzah are the five women who stood boldly before the congregation and its leadership and demanded a portion of their father's, Zelophehad's, possessions. Notably, their mother is not even given a name in the text. Still, Mahlah, Noah, Hoglah, Milcah, and Tirzah maintained their father's inheritance intact among his immediate family even though he had no sons. Their case was appealed to the highest court in the land, the Supreme Court of the LORD, presented by Moses, establishing a precedent early in the history of the Israelites for women receiving their father's inheritance.[5]

The Black woman's biblical reading incorporates all the aforementioned characteristics. Being raised in the church, I can say that it was through the efforts of the women in my family. Because of the women in my family and community, I played active roles in church during my formative years. My mother and her mother ensured my siblings and I were in church every Sunday and that we participated in the youth choir and all other youth activities. More specifically, it was my mother, Irene, who not only allowed me to ask questions but also encouraged me to do so. When she could not answer my question about why we say that "we believe in the catholic church" every week when reciting the Apostles' Creed at our Christian Methodist Episcopalian (CME) church, she told me to ask the pastor.

During my time in seminary, Dr. Chanequa Walker Barnes introduced me and others to Womanist Theology. She helped me to realize that Womanism informs my theology. I learned it was okay to read the Bible critically and with a hermeneutics of suspicion. It was the tool of the hermeneutics of suspicion that my mother enabled within me and my siblings.

One epiphany I learned in seminary was that the Black woman is one of the most oppressed people who read the Bible with the most hope. It is profound but indicative of the courage and the strength that is the faith of the Black woman. Black women's experiences of enslavement, marginalization, and oppression have uniquely shaped their engagement with the world, especially with the Bible. Many Black churches today owe their very existence to the Black woman's tenacity. I have witnessed Black churches without pastors during the COVID pandemic, whose women held them together for anywhere from several months to a couple of years. Historically, African American women have drawn inspiration from biblical figures like the Old Testament's strong matriarchs and the New Testament's courageous women. These stories have provided a foundation for Black women to navigate societal challenges and find hope amid adversity. Womanist Theology helps the Afrodiasporan reader center the voices, experiences, and concerns of Black women in their interpretation of scripture. By affirming the lived realities of Black women, Womanist Theology challenges dominant narratives and offers a more inclusive and holistic approach to biblical interpretation.

Using a Womanist Theological lens, we can explore biblical narratives, focusing on the experiences and contributions of Black women and other marginalized people in the text. For example, the story of the Exodus liberation narrative takes on new significance when we consider the roles of Black women, such as Moses' mother, who risked her life and gave up her infant son to save him. We cannot forget Moses' sister Miriam, who led the recently liberated Israelite women in songs of celebration and resistance. By centering these women's perspectives, Afrodiasporan readers can glean insights into the intersection of race, gender, and liberation throughout the biblical text. Womanist Theology invites us to critically examine biblical texts that have been used historically to marginalize others or reinforce patriarchal norms. In interrogating these texts, Afrodiasporan readers can reclaim their agency and not only challenge but destroy oppressive interpretations that have excluded or silenced Black women's voices.

The origins of Womanist Theology are deeply intertwined with the legacy of Black women's leadership and activism in liberation movements. Black women have played and continue to play pivotal roles in struggles for civil rights, gender equality, and social justice. Their experiences of intersectional oppression have informed their interpretations of the Bible, giving rise to Womanist Theology as a liberating framework.

Notable Womanist theologians, such as Dr. Emilie Townes, Dr. Jacquelyn Grant, Dr. Katie Geneva Cannon, and Dr. Delores S. Williams, have significantly contributed to Afrodiasporan biblical interpretation. Their scholarship emphasizes Black women's experiences, challenges oppressive scripture readings, and highlights the importance of community, justice, and freedom. Additionally, figures like Christena Cleveland, Ph.D., and her book *God is a Black Woman* have further deepened the exploration of Womanist Theology, offering a powerful perspective on the divine image of Black women and their role within religious and social contexts.

Historical figures like Jarena Lee (1783-1864), Maria Stewart (1803-1879), and Julia Foote (1823-1900) were trailblazing Black women preachers who made significant contributions to the religious landscape with their unique theological insights. Their voices challenged the prevailing norms of their time, laying the foundation for developing Womanist Theology. Harriet Tubman (1822-1913), an iconic figure of freedom and resistance, played a crucial role in the Underground Railroad and embodied Womanist theological principles. Tubman's deep faith and commitment to liberation for her people intertwined with her understanding of God's call to justice and equality, reflecting a form of Womanist Theology in practice. Although a devout Christian, Harriet Tubman was a bodhisattva in that she chose not to remain in paradise but went back into the midst of pain and suffering to rescue others.

Delores S. Williams' groundbreaking work in her book *Sisters in the Wilderness* explores Black women's experiences, struggles, and resilience. Williams examines the biblical narrative through a Womanist lens, emphasizing the importance of self-definition, self-affirmation, and self-determination for Black women in their interpretation of scripture. By embracing Womanist Theology, Afrodiasporan readers, not just Black women, can draw inspiration from the long legacy of Black women's contributions to biblical interpretation. Through the Black woman, the African Diaspora can find affirmation in its identities, struggles, and aspirations, reclaiming its rightful place within the biblical narrative as catalysts for change, advocates for justice, and bearers of divine wisdom.

[1] "James Brown – It's a Man's World Lyrics | Genius Lyrics," accessed December 1, 2023, https://genius.com/James-brown-its-a-mans-world-lyrics.

[2] Pauli Murray, *To Speak a Defiant Word: Sermons and Speeches on Justice and Transformation* (Yale University Press, 2023), 300, https://doi.org/10.2307/jj.4820344.

[3] Chanequa Walker-Barnes, *I Bring the Voices of My People: A Womanist Vision for Racial Reconciliation*, Prophetic Christianity (Grand Rapids: William B. Eerdmans Publishing Co, 2019), 12.

[4] Kimberle Crenshaw, "Mapping the Margins: Intersectionality, Identity Politics, and Violence against Women of Color," *Stanford Law Review* 43, no. 6 (1991): 1244, https://doi.org/10.2307/1229039.

[5] Wilda C. Gafney, *Womanist Midrash: A Reintroduction to the Women of the Torah and the Throne*, vol. First edition (Louisville, KY: Westminster John Knox Press, 2017), 156–57, https://search.ebscohost.com/login.aspx?direct=true&db=nlebk&AN=1571341&site=ehost-live&scope=site.

CHAPTER SIX

Black Queer Theology and the Bible: A Heteronormative Black Man's Perspective

***

"The theology of those at the center of society often seeks to characterize people on the edge as enemies of God. This is especially true when individuals or groups unrepentantly refuse to conform to the dominant definition of normativeness. Overcoming internal and external oppressive theology, or a theology that excludes certain people, is primary in creating a Christian community for people visibly on the periphery."
-Bishop Yvette A. Flunder[1]

***

Disclaimer: As a heteronormative man, I do not claim complete understanding of the plight of my Black Queer brothers and sisters. I am writing this to express solidarity with the Black Queer community, believing they are equal in the eyes of God and should be seen as equal in the eyes of humanity. I am sharing what I have learned and observed. I believe our heteronormative society, especially the Black Church, has much work to do to be open, inviting, and affirming to all, without exception. My goal is not merely to be an ally; I aim to be a co-conspirator in the fight against oppressive Christian doctrine and dogma.

I acknowledge that growing up in the South in the 1970s, I did not witness to a lot of homophobic behavior in my little corner of the world. My parents did not raise me that way. I grew up during a time when there were things that we did not openly discuss, like sexuality. This has nothing to do with queerness, but as a point of reference for the times I grew up in, I remember a family that lived up the street from us that had a family member who was born with a deformity. She was hidden away in a room. When we would visit with my friends at the house, the door to her room remained closed. I can honestly say that for all the times I stepped foot in that house, I can only remember catching a glimpse of her once when someone came out of the room after feeding her. They never took her outside. We never asked questions or asked to see her. She just existed.

In terms of my early perspective on queerness, I have a cousin who grew up with us in the 70s and was queer. I remember hearing him being called a sissy and telling people to "shut up" and chasing them for saying it. He was usually not around when they did this. His queerness did not stop us from playing with him and his younger brother when we went out to Big Momma's house in the country. Playing with him was not unlike playing with any of my other cousins or friends. We rode bicycles, explored the countryside, and had foot races (he always outran all of us). I saw him just as my cousin and a family member. I do not remember being taught to see or treat people differently by my parents or any other adults in my family.

It was not until high school that the 20th-century view of queerness became more evident to me. My cousin and I did run in different friend circles, but in my involvement with the high school band, I had some interactions with him and a friend of his who was more openly queer than my cousin. My parents never told me not to play with or associate with my cousin. It was through this that I developed a more open viewpoint of hetero- and homosexual relationships. He was different, but he was my cousin. I did not fully understand it, but it was what it was.

In my early adulthood years, I could never fully buy into what Christians would say about queer people. This was a problem because it conflicted with what I was taught: that God loves everyone. What cemented my open and affirming perspective was having children. I would read stories of children being thrown out of their parents' houses because of their queerness and some of them committing suicide as a result. I imagined any of my children coming to me and saying that they were gay, and my only response being, "I love you, no matter what." I could never imagine treating my child, or anyone else, for that matter, in such a way that would lead them to think life was not worth living. I would never be an accessory to someone's suicide, no matter what. I decided my not understanding someone's humanity was not reason enough to ostracize them.

Besides, my wife, Cheryl, and I have a philosophy regarding practicing our faith. We say that when interacting with people, we will always do our best to default to love because that is the core value of the Christian faith.

This chapter is not meant to be an anthropological study of the Black LGBTQIA community. Instead, I aim to assist the Black Church in learning how to embrace these individuals' humanity and theological viewpoints. Black Queer Theology is a new and rapidly developing theology rooted in the experiences of Black LGBTQIA persons. It challenges traditional interpretations of scripture by highlighting the inherent dignity and worth of all of humanity, regardless of sexual orientation or gender identity. Black Queer Theology enables us to read the Bible critically and intentionally. It draws attention to biblical passages, affirms and celebrates diversity, love, and acceptance, and offers a fresh and inclusive understanding of the Bible's messages. I chose to focus on Black queerness because Black intersectionality with anything will always highlight "the least of these." I also chose to focus on Blackness because it is the core of my being; it is the core of our being.

In Western society, there is still a struggle with accepting and affirming someone if they do not fit into a binary heteronormative box. How arrogant of us to think that we know all there is to know about God's design of the human spectrum!

Knowing that the Bible is read across the spectrum of the world's population, the understandings and interpretations of the Bible must also be on a spectrum. Just as light and sound are spectral, so must our understanding of humanity and scripture be spectral. As a scientist, specifically a physicist, I sincerely appreciate light and sound spectrums. The human senses of sight and hearing detect light and sound. Our senses are tuned to only see or hear within a specific range of light and sounds. This means that what we see and hear does not indicate all light and sound spectrums. Some lights and sounds in each spectrum are undetectable to the human senses. The human eye is only tuned to a specific range of visible light. The human ear is only tuned to a specific range of audible sounds. But outside of this range are lights and sounds that our human senses cannot detect. Some people can only see specific colors even within the human range of sight. Even among colorblind people, there is a spectrum range for those who cannot distinguish between specific colors and those who see no colors. The takeaway is that just because we cannot see or hear something does not mean it does not exist; this is the foundation of faith.

To take the spectrum concept one step further, the light spectrum is a subset of the electromagnetic spectrum. The electromagnetic spectrum consists of light, radio waves, and radiation, all based on energy. Although we cannot see electromagnetic waves, we can see the evidence of interactions with electromagnetic waves.

Black Queer Theology exists outside of but also includes the spectrums of mainstream Evangelical theology, Black Liberation Theology, and even Womanist Theology. Black Queer Theology offers a fresh, inclusive perspective on the Bible that challenges traditional interpretations and opens new possibilities for Afrodiasporan readers. I believe this is what draws me to Black Queer Theology because I have always gone against the grain when it came to religion and spirituality. The concept of being disruptive should make Black Queer Theology appealing to the Afrodiaspora. The disruptive nature of Black queerness is a prerequisite to true societal transformation. Douglas writes that we can only have transformation with "a sexual discourse of resistance."[2] Just as the Black LGBTQIA paradigm continues to expand as people discover they do not fit into one neat label or category, this should become the modus operandi for all theologies.

Black Queer Theology provides a framework, albeit amorphous, for exploring the intersection of sexuality, gender, and identity within the biblical text. Engaging with Black Queer Theology allows members of the Afrodiaspora to gain valuable insights that empower them to reclaim their full humanity and find liberation within the scriptures.

To fully understand the relevance of Black Queer Theology to Afrodiasporan biblical interpretation, we must recognize the complexities of sexuality, gender, and identity within the biblical context. The Bible reflects a diverse range of human experiences, including those related to sexual orientation, gender identity, and non-conforming expressions of sexuality and gender. When talking about sexuality and gender, Christians tend to lump them all together into one broad category—a taboo never to be spoken of openly. Evangelical Christians do not want to consider that there was more to the intimate relationships between Ruth and Naomi or David and Jonathan.

Let us examine a scripture passage that has historically been used to marginalize, oppress, and ostracize Black LGBTQIA individuals and explore how Black Queer Theology might offer new insights and perspectives for African American readers. We will look at the story in the 19th Chapter of Genesis. In the story, we find Lot and his family living in Sodom when he is approached by two guests, angels sent by God to get Lot and his family out of the city before it is destroyed.

White mainstream Eurocentric evangelical theology misinterprets the story of Sodom and Gomorrah as God's condemnation of same-sex sexual relations.

Black Liberation Theology sees the story as one of redemption and hope in the face of doom and despair.

Black Queer Theology invites us to reconsider the narrative, exploring the theodicy of God, the nefarious nature of man, and the social injustice present in the text.

By examining the story through a Black Queer theological lens, Afro-diasporan readers can uncover the underlying messages of hospitality, radical inclusivity, and justice, challenging oppressive interpretations.

Black Queer Theology challenges traditional interpretations of scripture by highlighting the inherent dignity and worth of not just LGBTQIA individuals but of all humanity. It calls into question heteronormative assumptions and encourages readers to consider alternative understandings of biblical passages. Dr. Kelly Brown Douglas states,

It is vital for Black and Womanist theologians to engage in and promote a sexual discourse of resistance not only because of the need to restore the relationship between human sexuality and the God of Jesus Christ but also to connect the Black faith with its "authentic religious heritage and to liberate Black people from the cycle of White cultural sin.[3]

By embracing Black Queer Theology, African American readers can challenge oppressive systems of interpretation that have excluded or marginalized not only Black voices but Black LGBTQIA voices. Embracing Black Queer Theology is not like performing "Conversion Therapy" on queer teens. From what I have learned and observed about "Conversion Therapy," there is nothing therapeutic about it for the ones subjected to it. They are made to feel as if they are less than human and are not really who they are. Embracing Black Queer Theology is not about converting a heteronormative binary person into a queer person, just as embracing Black Liberation Theology is not about converting a queer person into a heteronormative person. Reading the Bible through a Black Queer lens does not mean that you deny who you are as a heteronormative binary person. It means that we can read the Bible with more of an egalitarian mindset, without the typical dividing lines of sexuality and gender.

Furthermore, Black Queer Theology offers new insights for African American readers by affirming the diversity and complexity of human experiences. It allows for a more inclusive understanding of biblical narratives and characters, recognizing the presence and contributions of LGBTQIA individuals within the biblical text. This expanded perspective fosters empathy, compassion, and a deepened appreciation for the full spectrum of human experiences.

I can imagine reading the Abraham, Sarah, and Hagar story. From a white Eurocentric mainstream evangelical perspective, Hagar is seen as being disrespectful and disobedient because God chose Abraham and Sarah. Abraham and Sarah are seen as the protagonists, while Hagar is an extra in the movie. Looking at it from a Womanist perspective, you may see Hagar as a rape victim. Womanist Theology acknowledges that her womanhood was violated but disregarded because of the context in which the story occurs. Looking at it from a Black Queer perspective, you may see Abraham and Sarah as the ones who did not trust God. They chose to take matters into their own hands, resulting in Ishmael. A Black Liberation theologian might focus on the enslavement of Hagar and draw parallels to the period of the Atlantic slave trade. A Womanist may see Hagar's story as one of a woman who had to forfeit her agency because of her enslavement, sacrificing her womanhood. A Black Queer theologian might see Hagar as a woman who was not allowed to live in her own gender identity and sexual orientation. What if Hagar never wanted to have children or even be with a man sexually? We then can see this story as a violation of not only her civil rights but her humanity as well.

Engaging with Black Queer Theology allows African American readers to find liberation and affirmation within the biblical text and in life. It provides a framework for understanding their experiences, identities, and relationships in consideration of scripture. Black Queer Theology invites not only Black Queer Bible readers but all Black Bible readers to embrace their authentic selves, challenge societal norms, and promote a theology of radical love and acceptance. By centering the voices and experiences of Black queer persons, Black Queer Theology offers unique insights that illuminate the biblical text and empower all Afrodiasporan readers in their spiritual journeys.

The takeaways are that reading the Bible from a Black Queer perspective helps us live a more spiritually fluid life, fostering selflessness. We can fulfill the Two Greatest Commandments through compassion and empathy: to love the LORD God with all our heart, mind, and soul and to love our neighbors as ourselves. We will be more likely to see people who are not like us as one of us.

I am heterosexual because you are homosexual. I am a heteronormative man because you are a transgender woman. I am because you are. You are because I am. I am because we are. We are because I am. This is UBUNTU.

[1] Yvette A. Flunder, *Where the Edge Gathers: Building a Community of Radical Inclusion*, electronic resource (Cleveland: Pilgrim Press, 2020), 16, https://www.galileo.usg.edu/redirect?inst=cts1&url=http://search.ebscohost.com/login.aspx?direct=true&scope=site&custid=cts1&authtype=ip,shib&db=nlebk&db=nlabk&AN=2376649.

[2] *Sexuality and the Black Church: A Womanist Perspective a Book by Kelly B Douglas*, 2003, loc. 1974 of 2942, https://bookshop.org/p/books/sexuality-and-the-black-church-a-womanist-perspective-kelly-b-douglas/630063.

[3] *Sexuality and the Black Church*, loc. 2213 of 2942.

CHAPTER SEVEN

Integrating Perspectives: Reading the Bible Holistically

This chapter will explore the transformative power of integrating Black Liberation, Womanist, and Black Queer theologies to read the Bible from a holistic African American perspective. We will delve into the interconnectedness and complementarity of these theological frameworks and discuss their relevance in a post-COVID, post-truth, and post-Christendom era. Additionally, we will consider the decline in support for evangelicalism and reflect on the potential of Artificial Intelligence (AI) and Afrofuturism in shaping the Afrodiaspora's relationship with scripture.

Let's explore the latter first.

AI and Afrofuturism offer unique possibilities for the Afrodiaspora to engage with the Bible and envision a future and present that centers their experiences, hopes, and aspirations. Afrofuturism, an artistic and cultural movement that emerged in the 20th century as a response to the historical erasure of Black people and their contributions in a future society, embraces the intersections of technology, culture, and spirituality to imagine alternative futures where Black voices are centered and empowered. Although I am discussing concepts that seemingly have a futuristic connotation, it does not equate to imprisoning the Black psyche in waiting for deliverance in the "Sweet By and By." The four centuries of pain and suffering on Earth were so great, so awful for the African Diaspora that Black Christianity could only assure reprieve in the afterlife. For so long, the dream of streets of gold and residence in one of God's many mansions led to earthly silence in the face of injustice and a faith that failed to challenge the dehumanization of Black bodies.[1] Western Christianity has long provided comfort for the Afrodiaspora but has been impotent in properly chiding the white malefactor. This is not about blaming the victim but more about blaming the victim's religion. Black Liberation, Womanist, and Black Queer theologies push the faith of the Afrodiaspora to play a more active role in the community. From a religious perspective, Artificial Intelligence and Afrofuturism offer hope for envisioning a future where the entirety of the African Diaspora is valued and fully seen. Afrofuturism celebrates Black culture, spirituality, and resilience, presenting a vision of liberation and self-determination, encouraging the Afrodiaspora to reclaim its narrative and imagine a future that embraces its inherent worth and dignity.

It allows us to see beyond the despair of characters like Hagar and acknowledge that she was one of the first non-Israelite people whom God chose to interact with and include in a covenantal promise. God assured Hagar that Ishmael would be heir to a generational blessing, akin to that of Abraham. Although Abraham's son Ishmael was blessed with twelve sons, the realization of Abraham's blessing would come a generation later through his grandson Jacob (Israel). A blessing delayed was not a blessing denied. The blessing of Ishmael would later be acknowledged in the faith of Islam. Interestingly, Abraham's promise through the intended path of Isaac was tortuous and fraught with scandal, much like the religion of whiteness.

In biblical interpretation, AI can assist in uncovering hidden meanings and connections within scripture. Advanced algorithms and computational analysis can help explore the complexities of biblical texts, shedding light on nuanced interpretations and highlighting marginalized voices that have been historically sidelined. Artificial Intelligence can ask and answer questions we have been discouraged from raising. It is not about viewing AI as God but as a tool to enhance interaction with Afrodiasporan religion and spirituality.

The metaphysical reality for African Americans in the United States is marked by the ontological concerns posed by continued dehumanization and vilification of Black bodies. The deaths of George Floyd, Breonna Taylor, and countless other Black men and women at the hands of law enforcement have profoundly impacted the African Diaspora. These tragic events highlight the urgent need for our faith to play a more active role in confronting systemic racism and dismantling structures of oppression.

In the face of this reality, Afrofuturism and a holistic approach to biblical interpretation can serve as not only metaphysical but tangible sources of hope and resilience. They empower the Afrodiaspora to envision a future where justice, liberation, equality, and equity are realized. By embracing the interconnectedness of Black Liberation, Womanist, and Black Queer theologies and incorporating AI and Afrofuturism as tools for exploration and analysis, Afrodiasporan readers can navigate the challenges of their present reality while forging a path toward a more inclusive and equitable future.

From a religious perspective, Afrofuturism offers hope and empowers the African Diaspora to reclaim its narrative and imagine a future where Black people are not only seen but fully valued. Recognizing their interconnectedness and complementarity, engaging in community dialogue, and adopting a holistic approach to biblical interpretation allow us to navigate the complexities of our world and envision a future grounded in justice, liberation, and equality.

Additionally, integrating AI and Afrofuturism into Afrodiasporan faith opens new possibilities and helps grapple with the ontological concerns of the continued dehumanization, vilification, and lynching of Black bodies. Embracing a holistic approach to biblical interpretation and drawing from the rich theological traditions of Black Liberation, Womanist, and Black Queer theologies, the African Diaspora can find strength, resilience, and inspiration to confront these challenges and work towards a more inclusive and equitable society.

So, what is the importance of what I have covered in this book? I have heard from so many people about being on a deconstruction journey, but I am still waiting to hear from someone about being on a reconstruction journey. Part of the problem is that, depending on the amount of deconstruction, there might be very little left to build upon. This is particularly true for members of the African Diaspora, as faith has played such a critical role in our lives. The Black Church has been the hub of activities ranging from feeding the hungry to serving as a training ground for civil rights activism. The question is whether the Black Church is still capable of fulfilling these roles, along with providing spiritual care to its attendees.

My hope for this book is also for those who are not members of the Afrodiaspora to use the teachings from these theologies to create a more inclusive, open, and affirming environment for the Black bodies that may be sitting in their pews. I also hope that the African Diaspora takes these theologies and works toward dismantling the oppressive structures within Black communities and especially within the Black Church. Embracing these theologies will help give us a new self-consciousness, a heightened sense of being and self-love.

As Zoom meetings, FaceTime, and other digital platforms have become more prevalent in faith because of the COVID pandemic, and as many individuals choose not to return to brick-and-mortar churches, hybrid church settings need to embrace more creative ways of teaching and utilize social media to disseminate teachings effectively. The pandemic has proven to be disruptive and disembodying for a community that has depended so much on proximity and touch in its faith.

The shift to an increasingly hybrid environment during and following the COVID pandemic posed challenges and created opportunities for biblical interpretation from an Afrodiasporan perspective. As individuals engage in online platforms for religious gatherings, the traditional dynamics of in-person church experiences have changed. However, this new landscape opens space for innovative and creative worship experiences. Hybrid church settings must be open to exploring new ways of delivering teachings through digital platforms, utilizing social media to disseminate messages, and fostering interactive online communities.

Social media platforms offer unique opportunities to reach a broader audience and engage in meaningful conversations about biblical interpretation. Platforms like Twitter, Instagram, and YouTube allow Afrodiasporan perspectives to be shared with individuals who may not have access to traditional church settings. Short video teachings, thought-provoking posts, and engaging discussions can spark curiosity and foster dialogue. Creative teaching methods, such as interactive webinars, online workshops, and virtual study groups, can help individuals actively engage with scripture and apply an Afrodiasporan perspective to their study and interpretation. These methods enable participants to connect with others, exchange insights, and better understand the ethical and social justice dimensions embedded within Black Liberation, Womanist, and Black Queer theologies. What might come out of religious pop-ups occurring in venues outside of traditional and conventional church settings?

Incorporating elements from other faith practices, such as Buddhist meditation, Muslim prayers, Yoruba, and other African faith practices, can enrich spiritual direction and deepen one's connection with the Divine. These practices offer different prayer, meditation, and reflection approaches, allowing individuals to explore diverse spiritual paths while staying grounded in their Afrodiasporan identity. By drawing upon the wisdom and teachings of other faith traditions, the African Diaspora can expand its spiritual toolkit, embracing a holistic approach to personal spiritual wellness and wholeness. These practices can help foster a sense of interconnectedness, self-awareness, and mindfulness, creating a space for individuals to navigate the challenges of everyday life and seek a spiritual direction that aligns with an Afrodiasporan perspective.

An Afrodiasporan perspective on biblical interpretation remains highly relevant in contemporary contexts. As society grapples with issues of racial injustice, systemic oppression, and social inequality, the ethical and social justice dimensions embedded within Black Libera-tions, Womanist, and Black Queer theologies offer invaluable insights. These perspectives challenge oppressive systems, advocate for justice, and affirm the dignity and worth of all individuals, especially those within the African Diaspora.

By incorporating an Afrodiasporan perspective into personal spir-itual practice and community engagement, individuals can actively pursue individual healing and social transformation. This approach en-courages dialogue, empathy, and solidarity, fostering connections that transcend virtual spaces and contribute to the ongoing work of justice and liberation.

[1] James H. Evans, *We Have Been Believers: An Afrodiasporan Systematic Theology* (Minneapolis: Fortress Press, 1992), 16.

CHAPTER EIGHT

Conclusion

In this book, we have embarked on a journey to explore the transformative power of engaging with the Bible from an Afrodiasporan perspective. Throughout our exploration, we have uncovered vital points and gained valuable insights that have the potential to shape our understanding of scripture and its relevance to the lives of the members of the African Diaspora.

First and foremost, we have recognized the importance of reclaiming our voices and experiences as the African Diaspora in interpreting the Bible. By acknowledging our unique cultural and historical context, we bring fresh insights to the text, shedding light on its meaning in ways that resonate deeply with our communities.

UBUNTU and the Word emphasizes the significance of Black Liberation, Womanist, and Black Queer theologies in shaping a more inclusive and liberating interpretation of scripture. We need to know that they are not mutually exclusive, and someone may ascribe to multiple theologies depending on the space they might be occupying at any given moment. These theological frameworks empower us to challenge traditional, exclusionary readings of the Bible and explore alternative perspectives that celebrate diversity, justice, and equality. Incorporating these perspectives into our reading opens doors to a richer and more meaningful understanding of God's message of love and liberation.

One of the main goals of this book was to highlight the contemporary Afrodiasporan religious and spiritual experiences while affirming our various human identities. From the stories of liberation and resilience in Exodus to the prophetic call for justice in the words of Amos and Isaiah, we have found a profound connection between the Bible and our struggles for freedom and equality. These passages remind us of our collective strength and inspire us to continue our pursuit of justice and righteousness.

As I conclude this book, I want to encourage readers to continue exploring and engaging with the Bible from the entire African Diasporan perspective. The journey does not end here; it is an ongoing process of discovery and transformation. It allows us to dive deeper into the rich tapestry of African American biblical interpretation, seek out the works of Black Liberation, Womanist, and Black Queer theologians, and engage in dialogue with others who share a passion for a more inclusive understanding of scripture.

Remember that the transformative power of reading the Bible from an Afrodiasporan perspective extends far beyond our individual lives. As we embrace our unique vantage point, we contribute to the broader narrative of the theological and spiritual development of the entire African Diaspora. We become agents of change, reshaping the Afrodiasporan spiritual narrative in a post-COVID, post-truth, and post-evangelical United States.

In closing, let us celebrate the richness and diversity of the African Diaspora, embracing the transformative power of Black Liberation, Womanist, and Black Queer theologies. Doing so unlocks new dimensions of understanding, empathy, and love. May this book guide your ongoing journey of exploring the Bible as an African American, and may it inspire you to embrace your identity, engage in critical reflection, and shape a more inclusive and liberating interpretation of scripture for ourselves, our communities, and our future generations.

WORKS CITED

Barreto, Eric D., editor. *Thinking Theologically: Foundations for Learning*. Fortress Press, 2015.

Danxu, Yang. "World's Largest Bible Printer Hails from Atheist China." *ThinkChina*, 2 Dec. 2019. http://www.thinkchina.sg/worlds-largest-bible-printer-hails-atheist-china.

"Bible Belt." *Merriam-Webster.com Dictionary*, Merriam-Webster, https://www.merriam-webster.com/dictionary/Bible+Belt. Accessed 27 Dec. 2022.

Brown, James, and Betty Jean Newsome. Lyrics to "It's a Man's World." *Genius*, https://genius.com/James-brown-its-a-mans-world-lyrics. Accessed 1 Dec. 2023.

Bynum, Edward Bruce. *Our African Unconscious*. 2021. https://www.simonandschuster.com/books/Our-African-Unconscious/Edward-Bruce-Bynum/9781644113967.

Digital Public Library of America. "Family Bible Records as Genealogical Resources." https://dp.la/news/family-bible-records-genealogy/. Accessed 19 Aug. 2023.

Ethoke, Nathalie. *Black Existential Freedom*. Rowman & Littlefield Publishers, 2023.

Evans, James H. *We Have Been Believers: An Afrodiasporan Systematic Theology*. Minneapolis: Fortress Press, 1992.

Ford, David F., editor. *The Modern Theologians: An Introduction to Christian Theology in the Twentieth Century*. 2nd ed. Blackwell, 1997.

Gafney, Wilda C. *Womanist Midrash: A Reintroduction to the Women of the Torah and the Throne*. 1st ed. Westminster John Knox Press, 2017. https://search.ebscohost.com/login.aspx?direct=true&db=nlebk&AN=1571341&site=ehost-live&scope=site.

Heick, Terry. "What Is Critical Reading? A Definition For Learning." *TeachThought*, 8 March 2022. https://www.teachthought.com/literacy/what-is-critical-reading-definition/.

Helios Publishing. *James Baldwin's Little Book of Selected Quotes*.

Hornsby, Teresa J., and Ken Stone. *Bible Trouble: Queer Reading at the Boundaries of Biblical Scholarship*. Society of Biblical Literature, 2011.

"I'm Just a Nobody Lyrics - Google Search." Accessed September 1, 2023. https://www.google.com/search?client=safari&rls=en&q=i%27m+just+a+nobody+lyrics&ie=UTF-8&oe=UTF-8.

Kirrsch, Irwin S., et al.. "Adult Literacy in America."

Lamb, Richard, and William Taylor. Lyrics to "I Wish I Knew How It Would Feel To Be Free." *Genius*, https://genius.com/Nina-simone-i-wish-i-knew-how-it-would-feel-to-be-free-lyrics. Accessed 6 Dec. 2023.

McGrath, Alister E. *In the Beginning: The Story of the King James Bible and How It Changed a Nation, a Language, and a Culture.* 1st ed. Doubleday, 2001.

Murray, Pauli. *To Speak a Defiant Word: Sermons and Speeches on Justice and Transformation.* Yale University Press, 2023. https://doi.org/10.2307/jj.4820344.

"National Cathedral's Confederate-Themed Stained Glass to Be Replaced with Racial Justice Imagery to 'Tell the Truth' of Country's Past - CBS News," 24 Sept. 2021. https://www.cbsnews.com/news/national-cathedral-confederate-stained-glass-replaced-racial-justice-imagery/.

National Council on Family Relations. "Inclusion and Diversity Committee Report: What's Your Social Location?" https://www.ncfr.org/ncfr-report/spring-2019/inclusion-and-diversity-social-location. Accessed 24 Aug. 2022.

Pocket Dictionary of Biblical Studies: Over 300 Terms Clearly & Concisely Defined. https://www.christianbook.com/dictionary-biblical-studies-clearly-concisely-defined/arthur-patzia/9780830814671/pd/14674. Accessed 26 Aug. 2022.

Polk, David. "Toni Morrison On Writing Without the 'White Gaze' | American Masters | PBS." American Masters, 18 June 2020. https://www.pbs.org/wnet/americanmasters/toni-morrison-on-writing-without-the-white-gaze/14874/.

Prince. Lyrics to "Let's Go Crazy." *Genius.* https://genius.com/Prince-and-the-revolution-lets-go-crazy-lyrics. Accessed 29 Nov 2023.

Riley, Cole Arthur. "God of the Black Woman." The Presbyterian Outlook, 17 May 2022. https://pres-outlook.org/2022/05/god-of-the-black-woman/.

Rogers, Andrew P. *Congregational Hermeneutics: How Do We Read?* Routledge, 2016. https://doi.org/10.4324/9781315562995.

Spong, John Shelby. *Biblical Literalism: A Gentile Heresy: A Journey into a New Christianity through the Doorway of Matthew's Gospel.* 1st ed. HarperOne, 2016.

Task, Allison. "What Is Ubuntu Philosophy & What Can We Learn From It? - Allison Task." 23 Feb. 2023. https://allisontask.com/ubuntu-philosophy/.

Thomas, Frank A. *Introduction to the Practice of African American Preaching.* Abingdon Press, 2016.

"Translation Reading Levels." *Christianbook*, https://www.christian-book.com/page/bibles/about-bibles/bible-translation-reading-levels. Accessed 24 Aug. 2022.

Walker-Barnes, Chanequa. *I Bring the Voices of My People: A Womanist Vision for Racial Reconciliation.* Prophetic Christianity. William B. Eerdmans Publishing Co, 2019.

Warren, Calvin L. *Ontological Terror: Blackness, Nihilism, and Emancipation.* Duke University Press, 2018.

"What Is the Bible Belt? Know the States, History, and Beliefs." https://www.christianity.com/church/the-bible-belt.html. Accessed 30 Aug. 2023.

"What We Can Learn from the African Philosophy of Ubuntu - BBC REEL - YouTube." https://www.youtube.com/. Accessed 31 Aug. 2023.

AUTHOR BIO

Corey was born in the small town of Quitman in South Georgia to James C. and Irene Brown. Early on, his family instilled a strong belief in God. Corey took this strong foundation wherever he went, and following high school, he took God with him into the US Navy. He received a Bachelor of Science in Physics from Florida State University and a Master's Degree from the US Air Force's Air Command and Staff College. During his service in the Navy, he regularly attended church no matter the duty station and served tirelessly. Even while underway on submarines, he was designated a Protestant lay leader and held prayer services for crewmembers on Sunday mornings. Corey's passion for teaching was instrumental in teaching youth and adults Bible Study and Sunday classes. Before retiring from the Navy in 2011, he was ordained as a deacon at First Baptist Church of Lincoln Gardens in Tampa, FL.

After 24 years in the US Navy, he retired and dedicated himself full-time to Christian ministry, serving as interim pastor of St. Luke Baptist Church in Gainesville, GA. His love of the scripture and sharing with others is a motivating force in his love of ministry. He pastors a hybrid church plant, Hush Harbor Ministry, in Moultrie, GA. Corey graduated from McAfee School of Theology with a Master of Divinity in 2018. He is currently a Doctor of Ministry candidate at Columbia School of Theology in Atlanta, scheduled to finish in 2025. Corey is married to Cheryl, and they reside in Moultrie, GA, with their fur babies, Bella and Chloe. He has four children from a previous marriage: Shawn (38), Courtney (29), Cayla (25), and Chris (24).

Printed in the USA
CPSIA information can be obtained
at www.ICGtesting.com
JSHW011734140124
55278JS00014B/142